$5⁰⁰
prt
4/18

SONICS IN WARHOLIA

Megan Volpert

SiblingRivalryPress

Alexander, Arkansas

www.siblingrivalrypress.com

Sonics in Warholia

Author photo by Rob Friedman. Used by permission.

Cover design by Mona Z. Kraculdy.

Sibling Rivalry Press, LLC
13913 Magnolia Glen Drive
Alexander, AR 72002

www.siblingrivalrypress.com

Thanks to the editors of *Ariel*, *Black Warrior Review*, and *Trunk of Delirium* for their willingness to publish some form of the pieces that appear here.

Additional works of art that orbit this project, including audio companion and responses from other writers, can be found on the author's website (located predictably at www.meganvolpert.com).

ISBN: 978-1-937420-04-8

First Sibling Rivalry Press Edition, December 2011

portrait of a mix tape

for the love of good machines

illusion of depth and vanishing acts

photographs of stolen things

dear diary of a dead man's telephone number

of confessions during blow job

ballad of the maladies

recurring fear of flat champagne

Portrait of a Mix Tape

The purpose of a mix tape is to evoke certain feelings in the listener by archiving a set of songs the listener will for whatever personal reason associate with particular moments in time that are linked to these feelings. In general, the mix tape can be viewed as an emotional salve, either a soothing presence or a generator of energy and excitement. Occasionally however, the mix tape is meant to chart the entire course of a person's life, as a sort of greatest hits or magnum opus. Thusly, Andy, please enjoy your 58 years boiled down to fifty-seven minutes and fifty-one seconds.

But you cannot enjoy it; it's too suspenseful. You already sense the potential badness, the caughtness of moments meant to be filed far away. To temporarily allay your fears, we will begin with The Velvet Underground and Nico's "All Tomorrow's Parties," which is a tribute to you and supposedly your favorite song. But then it is followed crushingly with David Bowie's "Andy Warhol," also meant as a tribute to you that you nevertheless despised.

And what costume shall the poor girl wear to all tomorrow's parties? Andy Warhol looks a scream. She'll turn once more to Sunday's clown and cry behind the door. Hang him on my wall. For Thursday's child is Sunday's clown, for whom none will go mourning. Andy Warhol, Silver Screen, can't tell them apart at all.

7

"Mack the Knife," with lyrics originally composed by Bertolt Brecht for *The Threepenny Opera*, premiered the year you were born and has in common with "All Tomorrow's Parties" that it has been subsequently covered by every musician under the sun. The day you expired, Bon Jovi's "Livin' On A Prayer" was number one on the Billboard charts, as it had been since Valentine's Day of 1987. Bon Jovi's merchandise includes an eco-friendly "Warhol Heart and Dagger" t-shirt.

Gina dreams of running away. Just a jackknife has old MacHeath, babe, and he keeps it out of sight. You live for the fight when it's all that you've got. Fancy gloves, though, wears old MacHeath, babe, so there's never, never a trace of red. It's tough, so tough. Now on the sidewalk, sunny morning, lies a body just oozing life. It doesn't make a difference if we make it or not. Could it be our boy's done something rash? We've got each other and that's a lot for love. Five will get you ten, old Macky's back in town. We'll give it a shot. Yes, that line forms on the right, babe, now that Macky's back in town. We're half way there, living on a prayer. Look out, old Macky is back!

In 1964, you did the cover art for John Wallowitch's album *This is John Wallowitch*. In the song "I See the World Through Your Eyes," Wallowitch has a conversation with his late brother, Edward, who worked with you as a photographer. Lou Reed wrote a similar conversation with you, called "Andy's Chest," that appears on the *Transformer* album produced by David Bowie, in between the songs "Vicious" and "Perfect Day."

If the last time you were here things were a bit askew, well, you know what happens after dark when rattlesnakes lose their skins and their hearts, and all the missionaries lose their bark. And even though I know you're gone and I'm wrong, I still expect to see your face in the throng and I still see the world through your eyes. Kingdom's Christian soldiers, dear, for you. You're living somewhere inside of me. Curtains laced with diamonds, dear, for you. And I still hear the sound of your voice.

A mix tape can be organized chronologically or thematically, depending on the best method of achieving maximum emotional effect. Especially when meant to address an entire life span, the tape can and should utilize both of these structuring principles.

Despite Mick Jagger's incomparable aloofness, you did two covers for The Rolling Stones as a means of amusing Bianca Jagger. In 1971, it was *Sticky Fingers*, whose giant, iconic hard-on pressing up against tight blue jeans pretty well sums up your thoughts on several subjects. Then for *Love You Live*, in 1977, it was a lame pastel scribble. You knew Bianca and Mick were on the verge of divorce then? From these albums, I've selected "Wild Horses" and of course "Sympathy for the Devil."

Please allow me to introduce myself: I'm a man of wealth and taste. You know I can't let you slide through my hands. Use all your well-learned politesse or I'll lay your soul to waste, um, yeah. Let's do some living after we die, because wild horses couldn't drag me away. Just as every cop is a criminal and all the sinners saints, as heads is tails, just call me Lucifer because I'm in need of some restraint. Childhood living is easy to do. I shouted out, "who killed the Kennedys," when after all it was

A mix tape often does not have enough reel on one side to accomodate the final song on that side with precision. This can be a frustrating experience for the listener because it prevents closure with a song and its accompanying memories. Please flip to Side B.

You produced and appeared in two music videos, Andy. The "Hello Again" video features you as a tuxedoed bartender for The Cars, along with a then-unknown Gina Gershon sticking out her tongue. The video for Curiosity Killed the Cat's "Misfit" features you knocking off Bob Dylan's "Subterranean Homesick Blues" promo video by dropping blank cue cards in time to the beat.

Sensitive child, keep running wild in a confined space. You just want to fly. How long, how low, how high can you go? You don't want to know it. Well, I can see the sorrow in your eyes. You want to call a truce. Sensitive child, your threat is so mild it worries me. Oh, you passed on mercy. Crazy sheep, you are the odd one out. I know you're a dreamer who's under the gun. This may come as some surprise. You left the scene without a trace, one hand on the ground, one hand in space.

There are at least two avant-garde bands that have been strongly influenced by you with a result that is almost despairingly creepy. There's nothing else to say except brace yourself, then take a listen to Devo's "Whip It" and Polkadot Cadaver's "Bring Me the Head of Andy Warhol."

Are you happy now? Try to detect it. Malevolence breeds contempt into a devious crush. Now whip it into shape. This is beginning to feel just like a competition. When a good time turns around, you must whip it. Fifteen minutes of fame is now the name of the game. Give the past the slip. Snapshots and flashbulbs ignite along the runway, and you freeze like a pale mannequin, I think you like what you see. No one gets away until they whip it. You have not even seen the last of me. When a problem comes along, you must whip it. Bring me the head of Andy Warhol. When something's going wrong, you must whip it. One day they'll find me with a candle burning inside of your skull. You will never live it down unless you whip it.

But I don't want to end on a down note, Andy. There are a number of musicians who are doing work that is totally sleek and sexy, very pop stuff that you should definitely approve. Celebrity is fashionable once more, and there is this new teen music scene known as "emo" that I think you could really get into. To update you on these developments, I'll finish the tape with two modern superstars. Here is Fall Out Boy with "This Ain't A Scene, It's an Arms Race" and Lady Gaga with "Paparazzi." Fall Out Boy has a "Warhol" t-shirt that is even weaker than Bon Jovi's, and bassist Pete Wentz repeatedly compares himself to you in interviews. So does Lady Gaga, whose Haus of Gaga arguably does in several ways resemble your Factory entourage.

Not sure what it means, but this photo of us, it doesn't have a price. Prima donnas of the gutter, at night we're painting your trash gold while you sleep. Ready for those flashing lights, because you know that, baby, I'm your biggest fan. That's just the business I'm in. We're plastic, but we still have fun. You look pretty sinking, but the real bombshells have already sunk. Baby, there's no other superstar. I don't really care which side wins, as long as the room keeps singing. Don't stop for anyone. Bandwagon's full, please, catch another. I'll chase you down until you love me. This ain't a scene, it's a god damn arms race.

So, there you go. Fourteen songs that scratch the surface. There is potentially enough room here at the end to add one more song, but let's not risk it. I think you will find the entire catalog of albums by The Killers very relevant and appealing for a number of reasons, so it would be impossible to narrow that down to only one piece for tucking in here. Just let me know if you have heard any of their albums, Andy, and I'll get you copies of whatever you're missing. Also, I know you love your Sony, but have you thought about getting an iPod?

For the Love of Good Machines

It doesn't matter if you went to bed with Lou; he thinks of you like a father now. How many times did he lope in having written nothing, but claiming ten songlets just to please you? Finger tips pressed together and flexing your creakier joints, you want to know why not fifteen instead. Was he crestfallen every time, or steely against your predictable impulse toward productivity? Lo and behold: now an elder statesman of rock, Lou has made over forty albums in fifty years. That's not even including compilations, collaborations or appearances. And he found time to do a few films. Andy, you reproduce yourself.

Perhaps the most awe-inspiring thing about a motorcycle is that what it is doing on the outside does not precisely correspond to what it is doing on the inside. The speed of the wheels is not the same as the speed of the engine. At a full stop, the wheels of the bike are stationary while the engine continues to turn over. Or with a heavy load, the wheels of the bike move slowly while the engine increasingly works overtime. The work of the engine is not the same as the engine's product, which is pure speed.

In the song "My House," released on *The Blue Mask* in 1982, Lou Reed reflects on how lucky his life has been and counts the three things that most contribute to this feeling: his writing, his motorcycle and his wife. He also refers to "a spirit of pure poetry." The song is a tribute to his late mentor, poet Delmore

Schwartz. Andy, you must be so jealous of how much credit he gave this influence, but then when you died, Lou wrote an entire song cycle about you. The *Songs for Drella* album beats one measly tune, doesn't it?

Lou says of Schwartz, "my Dedalus to your Bloom, was such a perfect wit." Daedalus was father to Icarus, and fashioned the wings with which the boy flew into the sun. But here, Stephen Dedalus and Leopold Bloom refer to the antiheroes of James Joyce's *Ulysses*. In the end, 1966 in New York City, Delmore Schwartz was so isolated that the staff of the Hotel Marlon did not discover his body for two days. Have you ever been alone for two whole days, Andy?

A bike moves forward, always forward. It speeds ever onward, giving a strong sense of progress, of mileage. But the true measure of a bike is not the speed it produces. Rather, consider the work of the engine. The engine does not move forward, it revolves. It remains in one place, repeating itself, circulating around itself as it propels its hive down the road and into the sunset. The true measure of a motorcycle is therefore the tachometer.

A tachometer measures a motor's revolutions per minute. It keeps count of the work process done by the engine. This is in contrast to an odometer, which can only evaluate the product— the speed of the wheels. Imagine that life is a comic book, and each person has a bubble floating over their head: a tachometer of human work processes. What exactly would it measure?

Did you push it to the limit, Andy? The most interesting thing about your placid neon face is the mystery of what is going on underneath it. The wheels aren't moving, but my breast plate picks up the distinctive hum of an engine vibration. It's like the sonic thump of the bass against your sternum at a stadium show. We cannot relax. People mistake this for anxiety, and we pretend that this is the case so they will leave us alone. We work alone. We work a lot. We work all the time. We have real anxiety when we cannot work. My engine wants on.

It makes total sense that you refer to your tape recorder as your wife. Most tape recorders during the 1950s and 60s had a tachometer. A tape recorder's wheels, the electronics that drive the tape, use the tachometer's signal to play the tape at proper speed. This signal is measured against another reference signal, such as a quartz crystal or alternating current. A comparison of the two frequencies drives the speed of the tape. The tape transport is said to be at speed when the tachometer signal and the reference signal match. Do you often look at the tiny white numbers rolling up into the skull of the recorder, dreaming they might somehow align with the pace of the speed freaks chattering in your office? As long as those numbers keep counting, you are at work. Is it glorious each time they reach 999 and begin from zero again?

If your wife is recording at speed, you reach 999 every 16 minutes and 39 seconds. Is she faithful? Is she indisputable voice and memory, overlooking all your foibles but catching every witty word? Revolving always around you, you can be working and feeling alone even when she is in the room. You would love driving a motorcycle, Andy. The machine can only do what you tell it to do, and then reproduce that gesture endlessly.

Lou Reed has a passion for motorcycling. Many bikes appear in his lyrics, and many bikers identify with his songs. In one song, his life is headed for the existential toilet bowl. He responds by aiming his bike directly at a fat pothole. Bottoming out is a term that refers to pushing a bike's suspension to its limit, causing a rough ride, preventing the wheels from adequately responding to the controls and significantly increasing the chance of a crash. The song "Bottoming Out" appears on the *Legendary Hearts* album, which Lou released in 1983. The album cover art displays a futuristic full-face helmet and a pair of black leather riding gloves. This album also features the song "Don't Talk to Me About Work."

We can all agree you should be on a bike, Andy, but it is time to ask that most practical of rhetorical questions: Harley or Honda? Have you ever seen a gutter ball pop inexplicably, rapturously out of its rut and knock down a bunch of pins? Despite this touching feeling that you are a proud American who can drive only an American-made bike, I have a much stronger compulsion to believe your bike of choice is made in Japan.

In the matter of speed, there is no contest. You cannot race on a Harley. But moreover, in the matter of your art—amidst Campbell's cans, Brillo boxes, portraits of stage and screen icons, Americana of all kinds—your Mineola motorcycle, produced in

1985. A replica of the revolutionary Honda CB750 Four: the street fighter class of bigger, faster, cheaper bikes first introduced in 1969 that, along with Marlon Brando and the Hells Angels, cost Harley the majority of its market share. At a top speed of 120 miles per hour, the CB750 Four results in a new motorcycling class: superbike. It stayed in production for 34 years, and sold 400,000 copies within the first ten years. That's more than the number of times you copied your portrait of Marilyn Monroe, Andy.

Plus, it could out-perform Bob Dylan's Triumph 500 in every way. European and American bikes are too butch for you. You meet the nicest people on a Honda. That's what the advertising said in the 1960s. In 1984, Honda began using rock stars to sell their line of scooters in the U.S. Grace Jones, Adam Ant and Devo all appeared in the new marketing campaign. Lou Reed also did one of Honda's commercials, a year after he released *Legendary Hearts* with motorcycle gear on the cover. One year after this Honda ad, you did the Mineola piece, even though the bike had been around for two and a half decades at that point. Lou influences you, too, doesn't he?

Lou with his electric shock and heroin, with his deep layers, his lovely unmanageable appetites that you wish to peel slowly and see. I wonder about what you two were trading, and if it was fair or if it should have been fair. Ready to explode, you patched his noise with Nico, a piece of German plastic. The Exploding Plastic Inevitable kept you in transit together. Did you nurse him through hepatitis in 1966, or leave him smoldering at the hotel like a pet dog?

I worry about this, because *All Tomorrow's Parties* is one of my least favorite songs on the first and only Velvet Underground album you produced—the thirteenth greatest album of all time, according to *Rolling Stone Magazine.* Is it your favorite song because it revolved around you? Everybody knew Nico couldn't sing, but you got your way and you got into all those parties. Your best girls always leave you for Bob Dylan, Andy, though they come back later once he's laid them down in a crash. Lou hung around, his nihilistic urban punk confessions glamorously lunar eclipsing Dylan's mild and melodic Midwestern folk songs at every conceivable turn.

So what if Dylan ended up as number two, between The Beatles and Elvis, on *Rolling Stone*'s top fifty immortals of rock? The Velvet Underground is ranked at number nineteen. No one suspected that through all of this pop carnage, it would be Lou Reed alone who came out alive. He claims the ghost in his house spelled out D-e-l-m-o-r-e on his Ouija board. It is rumored that Delmore Schwartz once said to him: "You can write—and if you ever sell out and there's a Heaven from which you can be haunted, I'll haunt you."

Lou is your superbike, Andy. When he fired you, was it a surprise? Studies show that the limits of peripheral vision in typical motorcycle lines of sight make no contribution to the traffic hazard, because more than 75% of all crash hazards are within 45 degrees of either side of straight ahead. Lou Reed himself quit The Velvet Underground not too much later, one year after the Honda CB750 Four came out.

Illusion of Depth and Vanishing Acts

American Psycho was just sitting on the shelf at my grandmother's house, left there in a stack of old books she got from somewhere. It fell anonymously on me like a star. This was maybe my sophomore year of high school, the controversy long since blown over and the feminists keeping quiet. When the novel was basically faithfully adapted for the screen my first year of college, it was directed by Mary Harron. She also directed *I Shot Andy Warhol*, but we don't always have to talk about that.

I am ranting on the fly more than a decade later, explaining to a buddy the various reasons why I am the person he knows who is most qualified to phone interview Bret Easton Ellis. We make it to the stage where I get an advance copy, but the publicist begins to hint at overbooking and the interview is ultimately swept away. I am surprised that I am not disappointed. An impressive portion of my life has been spent on the study of topics related to Ellis, and suddenly I find myself not very interested to meet him. His spectre grows larger and more haunting as we approach the date when he will be in town. Is this how you felt about Picasso? All you ever talked about was charming little Paloma.

I don't really understand the mechanics of recording a phone interview. The first publicly available device for recording sound was the phonograph, invented by Thomas Edison. He first used tin foil to record the sounds through a phonograph, but the impracticality of the foil's delicate composition soon led Edison to try wax cylinders instead. He licensed the cylinders from Alexander Graham Bell, inventor of your precious telephone. This resulted in modern day records, and the wax cylinders went out of production a few months after you were born.

Tin foil tends to transfer a tin taste to the food wrapped in it, which is why it was replaced with aluminum foil in the early twentieth century. In a random survey of my acquaintances where I ask them to tell me anything they know about aluminum foil, they invariably all begin the response in one of three ways: a serious description of how to cook opiates or crack, a satirical description of how to make a hat to hear aliens or radio waves, or a warning against putting it in the microwave though none of them can say exactly why this is dangerous.

In physics class my senior year, we built a Leyden jar out of some paper clips, aluminum foil and a pickle jar. The teacher rubbed some fur over a plastic pipe, then touched the pipe to the top of the jar to charge it. We all held hands and braced ourselves for the teacher to touch the top of the jar. When he did, nothing happened. We messed up the connection somewhere, and the charge leaked out through the glass, which is a dielectric. There was repeated revising of calculations, clammy forcible hand holding, and trying not to flinch each time the teacher touched the jar while we waited for it to shock us.

Technically, it is a lecture followed by a book signing, free and open to the public. It is marked on my calendar, and as the days go by, I become increasingly anxious about how bored I am with the prospect of unwrapping the gift of the author's actual existence. Not living in New York or Los Angeles, this is probably my best chance to ever be in the same room with him. It is not to be turned down lightly, but if I want to know Bret Easton Ellis, I just look at the surface of his books and there he is. Over the course of two days, I read the new book in about three hours. The audiobook is four hours long, and narrated by brat pack actor Andrew McCarthy.

Ellis published his first book, *Less Than Zero*, in 1985. You were at the launch party because you liked the title, though you did not read the book. When the book was turned into a movie in 1987, McCarthy played one of the main characters, Clay Easton. This is the film that famously broke Robert Downey Jr., who played junky Julian Wells. McCarthy has also narrated an assortment of children's books, and almost inexplicably, a series of Bible stories.

McCarthy has been sober since 1992. Downey Jr. has been sober since 2003. Whether Ellis is sober is less than clear. In all the promotional interviews, he keeps inviting people to his apartment that is Clay's apartment in the new novel, walking around barefoot and offering them Coke long pause or Diet Coke. He keeps repeating the same ideas in answer to different questions: that numbness is valid as a feeling, that the people who reject you and minimalism just don't get it, that he is a moralist pushing a narcissist to his limits. He keeps saying that the empire is over, that New York is over.

In your heyday from 1963 to 1967, you were in the Silver Factory. Speed freaks were plentiful, and the minute you saw what Billy Name had done to his apartment, you asked him to do it to your office. Wall to wall aluminum foil. All your best movies were at least partly filmed there. He fixed it up, even dragged in the famous red couch, then retreated to the darkroom bathroom and only came out at night. The day Billy was born, Tibet enthroned its fourteenth Dalai Lama. One day Billy just went away, but he left you a note: "Andy - I am not here anymore but I am fine. Love, Billy."

Edison also invented the first motion picture camera, and was one of the first inventors to use principles of mass production in a laboratory environment. Your fourth and final factory, at East 33rd Street and Madison Avenue, was previously an electricity substation for Consolidated Edison. In Edison's first movies, he didn't move the camera. In your first movies, neither did you. Edison's short film of two people kissing was the first on-screen kiss ever, and many judged it as pornographic. You made pretty much the same movie he did thirty-three years later, and it was still judged pornographic.

The first motion picture projection screens were embedded with silver so that they would be highly reflective. These were eventually supplanted by dielectric screens, which are cheaper and reflect light less predictably. Metallic screens are back in fashion because three-dimensional movies depend on polarizing the image differently for each eye. Instead of silver, these new screens are shot through with aluminum. When Paul Morrissey shot your *Frankenstein* movie in 1973, it premiered in Space-Vision 3-D. It has several scenes of violent sex or disembowelment that could be easily inserted into any Bret Easton Ellis novel. Yours was the first 3-D movie to be rated X by the MPAA.

Just looking at the screen is not enough to see an image in 3-D. It is the glasses that actually expose a film's extra dimensionality for the eye to read. They are polarized just like regular sunglasses can be polarized. Do you wear Ray-Bans, Andy, or imitations? Ray Ban was founded in 1937, the year you got your first camera. Wayfarers arrived in 1952, the year you won your first award, for graphics promoting a radio show called *The Nation's Nightmare*. Wayfarers are mentioned seven times in *American Psycho*. They are mentioned three times in *Rules of Attraction*, and three times in *Less Than Zero*.

Robert Downey Jr. once wore Wayfarer knockoffs by Oliver Peoples to the Oscars. He visited your museum in 1999 while filming *Wonderboys*, for which Bob Dylan won an Oscar for Best Song. Downey Jr. used to work as an installation piece at Area for ten dollars an hour plus free liquor. He sent a Gumby doll to you down a conveyor belt. Julian Wells lives at the end of the novel, but dies in a car crash at the end of the film. Ellis initially refused to see the movie because it took so many liberties with the story. After the revelation that McCarthy is doing the audiobook, film buzz becomes inevitable.

But would Robert Downey Jr. ever agree to reprise the role that ruined him? This is a tricky psychological situation that no doubt interests you, Andy. It's like the second coming of Edie Sedgwick. Those that are not in the know question why it matters, since Julian dies at the end of the first film. Ellis cleverly resurrects him to be killed again at the end of the new book, and also spends the first twenty pages of the new book criticizing the first film. The whole thing is about the movie business, which is the kind of thing the movie business loves to make movies about the most, and the book is so short that Ellis could do the adaptation himself in half a minute. The only novel he's written that has not been made into a movie is *Glamorama*. There is a character in this novel that only owns two books: the Bible and your *Diaries*.

There were just so many times the entire physics class could rally to care about the outcome of the experiment. It caught most of us off guard when the Leyden jar sent a wave of lightning through the hands and hearts of each of us in turn, quickly and stunningly. It hurt, and I did not like it. It was so sharp that my mind constructed a noise like thunder for my chest. The teacher said there might be some residual charge, so we obediently all held hands again and waited tensely for the star to fall on us one more time.

Remembering the Leyden jar incident calls up Lou and Edie, a time when electroshock therapy was fashionable. Addiction and disembowelment seem like things worth avoiding, things that pop out at you. When I think about my relationship to aluminum foil, it's about wanting to partake but then being unable to back out, about wanting to study electricity but then becoming electricity. Shopping carts at the grocery store conduct a shock pretty easily, but when I reach to pull a cart out from the row, I am unafraid. I imagine you and Ellis wearing the same sunglasses at his book release, blankly mouthing about nothing, happily stuck flat against silver, holding charge.

Photographs of Stolen Things

You never got Imelda Marcos, who was ugly anyway, but after over a year of monthly needling at the caviar club, you did get a green light for Her Imperial Majesty Empress Farah Diba. This was six months after having frantically hop scotched through Ford's White House avoiding her. Way to bring home the bacon, Andy.

Twelve Iranian baby steps toward your dream of the infinitely multiplying portrait, and two hundred grand under the mattress. Sixteen months later in the high fundamentalist tide, you get Princess Ashraf and a slap on the wrist from *The Village Voice* cover calling you a beautiful butcher for it. The Shah is exiled less than a year after you get the go ahead to do his portrait.

In the savvy eyes of your entourage, the Iran of July 1976 is the same essential scene as Mulholland Drive. When Ayatollah Khomeini returned as the Supreme Leader in 1979, Shah Pahlavi fled to Egypt and many of his citizens immigrated to the U.S. There are an estimated one million Iranian nationals living near UCLA today, and this area of the city is often referred to as Tehrangeles. It is more commonly known as Westwood.

The Pierce Brothers Westwood Village Memorial Park Cemetery is located on Glendon Avenue, next to the Westwood branch of the Los Angeles Public Library system. A lot of people you like are dead here, Andy. Two months after I was born and twenty years after you did her portrait, Natalie Wood accidentally drowned and was buried here. Her grave is a fifteen second walk from Marilyn Monroe's crypt, whose portrait you started silk-screening immediately following her death from acute barbiturate poisoning in 1962.

Rumor has it that Marilyn was buried in a million dollar diamond necklace. Diamonds are a girl's best friend, and you love them more than the next girl, Andy. That guide at the vault holding Iran's Crown Jewels said you know more about stones than Elizabeth Taylor. The year after Audrey Hepburn starred in *Breakfast at Tiffany's*, based on the novella of same title by Truman Capote, two idiots cracked the marble edifice of Marilyn's crypt where they considered breaking through five hundred pounds of concrete to steal this hypothetical necklace.

Two years after Marilyn sang about the necessity of sparkly things and two years before Truman published his story regarding same, there is a photograph of them dancing together at El Morocco. It was on East 54th between 3rd and Lex, and is now a 32-story set of luxury condos. The photo, taken in 1955, features a typically drunken Truman trying in vain to lead Marilyn as she towers over his five feet three inches and makes eyes at someone over her shoulder out of the frame, one of the nightclub's trademark white palms imposing conspicuously from the background.

Truman Capote died of liver disease complicated by multiple drug intoxication one month shy of his sixtieth birthday. It was hardly a surprise, but the disappointment of someone fading out on the brink of such a milestone is exceeded perhaps only by the distress of someone blinking out too soon. When Justin Hilbun was killed in an inexplicable one-car crash on a Sunday afternoon just before his thirtieth birthday, musical instruments all over Louisiana were startled to remember they could not play themselves. Every image held up at my brother's jazz funeral was perfect because Justin not only photographed pretty, but also was one of those rare birds whose pictures do justice to his total self. You will find nothing needing touching up in this case, Andy. I have two hundred prints of the young man, the tone of his stand-up bass at my wedding, a fleur de lis on my right ankle and the shadow of his ashes on lower Decatur scattered at the river edge of the Quarter.

Half of Truman's ashes are in a crypt at the Westwood cemetery, on the outside west wall of the Sanctuary of Tenderness. The other half of his ashes were sent off with those of his longtime lover, Jack Dunphy, at Crooked Pond on Long Island ten years later. Jack actually thought he had all the ashes, but the former Mrs. Johnny Carson secretly kept half to fulfill Truman's dying wish of being eternally bicoastal. Truman died in his bedroom at Joanne Carson's house, and she put her half of the ashes on the table by that bedside. When a picture clearly detailing the urn was printed in *People Magazine* sometime later, Jack found out he was missing half of Truman and never spoke to Joanne again. During a Halloween costume party at her home in Bel Air, Joanne's half of the ashes were stolen along with two hundred thousand dollars' worth of jewelry. The ashes were mysteriously returned six days later, at which point Joanne decided Truman would be safer at the Westwood cemetery with Natalie and Marilyn.

From Truman's crypt, you can throw a stone at the grave of Swifty Lazar, the superagent who put Spago on the map with his famously elite post-Oscar parties. Truman was likewise known for his equally exclusive annual Black and White Ball. He began hosting it in 1966, the same year *In Cold Blood* was published. It was Swifty who negotiated a deal for *In Cold Blood*, the pioneering nonfiction crime novel that became an international bestseller and markedly demonstrated Truman's interest in reportage of dubious veracity. Swifty was also associate producer of *The Thorn Birds* miniseries. My mother named me after the main character, a woman who spent sixty years seducing the family priest.

Among Swifty's many famous clients was Tennessee Williams, who complained of the life-long and very public rivalry between Truman Capote and Gore Vidal that "you would think they're running neck and neck for some fabulous gold prize." Vidal said that Truman "has tried, with some success, to get into a world that I have tried, with some success, to get out of," and when Truman died, he called it "a good career move." Swifty Lazar had nothing but friends, while Truman Capote made nothing but enemies. He was one person in your life that you never had to cause any trouble for, Andy, because trouble was always already on that scene when you arrived.

In fact, you sometimes liked to bail him out, didn't you? In the early Seventies there was his failure to produce a field report on The Rolling Stones for *Rolling Stone*. But nobody has an easy time with Mick, so that one may have been cause for sympathy. You ended up interviewing Truman, and the magazine took that instead. Then in the late Seventies there were the serials from *Answered Prayers*, which collection he never finished, depicting among many sacred socialite undiscussables the dysfunctional daily life of Babe Paley, who was his best friend. Boy oh boy, did you have to tap dance repeatedly to extricate yourself from that one. You have a mortal fear of making enemies, don't you, Andy? This is a crucial difference between you and Truman. He was too often compelled toward giving a lie, whereas you can be content to just say nothing.

Mick Rock, best known for his floating heads photo on the cover of Queen's album *Queen II*, took a photo of you with Truman in 1979 that says everything. Truman is a cerulean elf with a huge rainbow lollipop and his arm reaching up across your shoulders. You are in a Santa suit and sunglasses, holding your precious but ungainly dachshund, Archie. The background is green, the center is off, and you both look as terrible as usual. In the left margin there's a hand and a Polaroid camera, the product of which is no doubt idling in one of your thousand time capsules. But this photo makes evident how you and Truman think about each other. Truman is looking at your sideline snapper while you are looking at Mick Rock.

The same blue of that elf costume colors Truman's eyes in the portrait you did of him that same year, in exchange for publishing a conversational portrait in *Interview* every month for twelve months. He was even in the toilet with Lee Radziwill and Jackie O at that point, and you completely revived his career one last time. When he compiled the pieces and published them as *Music for Chameleons* in 1980, it spent an unprecedented sixteen weeks on the bestseller list. You got no credit and no royalties.

Truman celebrated with a facelift, foreshadowed by your nip and tuck job on his portrait. You chiseled and then washed him out so much he is nothing but a hat and eyes, nothing more than an intense tilt of the head that I know you were aching to replicate. The original spark appears in a controversial photo of Truman taken by Harold Halma in 1947, for the back cover of *Other Voices, Other Rooms*. It is a withering come hither that can only be described as faggy, thanks to which the book became a bestseller.

How often did you examine that photo, Andy? You moved to New York the following year, and in 1952 had your first show: *Fifteen Drawings Based on the Writings of Truman Capote* at the Hugo Gallery on 55th Street. Truman's mother called you a faggot, and despite your persistent fan mail, Truman did not attend the opening. But you got him back by skipping his funeral. He didn't go to your first show, and you didn't go to his last.

This is all hundreds of miles away from New Orleans or Monroeville. This is far gone from Truman's blanky on display in the Old Courthouse, long removed from Harper Lee's precocious little friend who could read at age five, well past pasty outcasts hungering to escape into a Mardi Gras whose mirage of unspoiled plumage they imagine in their closet cased youth, when graveyards held less death and more sexy mystery.

Dear Diary of a Dead Man's Telephone Number

When you leave a house, you can go back to the building and wax nostalgic. This was my bedroom. This was the door frame where I used to mark my height twice a year. This was the foyer where my father's casket rested for three days. These were the steps upon which I sat every afternoon, watching my mother work in the front yard. This was the spot where we scattered the ashes. This was the spot where we grew up and apart. This was the spot where I swore to myself I'd get out of here someday.

I have located two of your old phone numbers, Andy. My instinct was to program them into my phone, where they have been cohabitating peacefully with other data until a moment where I can think of a good use for them. It feels like they should only be summoned for an emergency, but I can't imagine what an appropriate situation might be in this case.

When Justin was killed, the family used his cell phone to text everybody with information about funeral arrangements. It is harrowing to receive text messages from a dead man. When Errin was killed, there was a voice memo found on her cell phone where Errin is reminding herself to tell her partner how much she loves him. After downloading the memo, he kept her phone for his personal use, but had the number changed. I still have Justin and Errin's numbers in my phone.

Your first house and original Factory, 1342 Lex in Carnegie Hill, was designed in 1889. It has three thousand square feet though it is only sixteen and a half feet wide, a four bed three bath on five stories. After fifteen years of living there with your mother, you leased it to Fred Hughes, until he bought it from your estate in 1989 for just under six-hundred thousand. When Fred died in 2001, it sold to some marketing execs for two and a half million. They sold it seven years later for just under six million. This gives new meaning to the idea of appreciation, don't you think?

I consider seven ways to approach making the call. The number is owned by Verizon. My heart pounds like there is a chance you might pick up the phone yourself. There are three increasingly shrill warning tones, followed by that oh so familiar voice from times of rotary, "I'm sorry, the number you have reached is not in service." I'm sorry, too. I want to connect with someone, Andy. I want to ask for a name and occupation, find out if they know who you are.

There is this friend of mine who knew Allen Ginsberg pretty well. He used to get calls on his land line from a private number that caller ID would not register. No heavy breathing, no scary insinuations, just an open silence on the other end. The guy swore it was Ginsberg checking in from the beyond, but I have trouble telling the difference between bullshit and genuine belief in this case.

On Errin's birthday, my wife called her cell number to find out what happened to it. Less than a year after her death, it was too soon, a digital interpretation of personhood informing my wife not simply that the number was not in service, but actually accusing her of dialing incorrectly. This birthday is just a few days after the one-year anniversary of Justin's death. The still disconnected number gives me a sense of peace for Errin, and an ounce of courage for Justin.

What broke the seal was my little brother's birthday. I searched my contacts list to dial him up and send my best, but an elderly man with a Hispanic accent answered the phone. In the cell phone age, there is no such thing as a wrong number. If you are not talking to who you want to be talking to, the number is dead, transferred into the hands of a stranger. People rarely answer another person's cell phone. This is not like calling the Factory, where any number of tangential acquaintances feels free to make the ringing stop.

Justin's number rings one and a half times, then I hang up. My wife assures me that some kind of error message may have been forthcoming a half ring later, and I hit redial after three painfully slow minutes of my heart inching up into my throat. Two rings brings a simple hello in a south Louisiana twang belonging to a young man just like so many times before that I believe through some kind of phone voodoo I am listening to my Lazarus. Flashing in on the Scooby-Doo ending where Patrick Duffy isn't really dead because Victoria Principal just spent a year dreaming it, I scream a little inside my own personal *Dallas* and hang up.

When I regain consciousness of the sensibilities of our modern age, I send a text message. Apologizing for hanging up, I identify the reason for my call, which I suppose is now to find out who is in possession of the digital identity of my dead friend, but was perhaps originally in the hope that the number is dead forever-- tiny little flakes of one and zero drifting gracefully off the edge of a satellite somewhere, angelic, destined never for earth-bound connectivity again.

The second Factory was originally a fire station, and your first proper work space from the mid to late Sixties. It was the fifth floor at 231 East 47th Street, which as you know no longer exists, though the Diamond District of course remains right next door. The two buildings occupying what was once your space are the famed Turtle Bay condos, which sell at about six-hundred thousand for a studio, and the Vanderbilt branch of the YMCA. While working at this location, in the winter of 1966 you took out an ad in *The Village Voice*, offering, "I'll endorse with my name any of the following: clothing, AC-DC, cigarettes, small tapes, sound equipment, ROCK 'N' ROLL RECORDS, anything, film, and film equipment, Food, Helium, Whips, MONEY; love and kisses Andy Warhol." The ad also lists the Factory telephone number, so I just kind of stumbled into it.

The mysterious fiend who has reanimated Justin's number returns my text. He addresses me by my full name, horrifically demonstrating that he has bothered to search my own digital identity. The man tells me he is a Deputy Sheriff, and scolds me for calling people just to hang up on them. Justin's number has gone to a law dog. I tell him to keep the streets safe so great young men do not die for nothing. He says will do and take care. I consider deleting the number, weighing whether to keep it in case of wanting to call again in ten years, or even in case of needing a Deputy Sheriff next time I am in New Orleans.

The second Factory number is also owned by Verizon. I call it seven times. Every time I call, I let it ring ten times, but there is no answer and no answering machine. It doesn't matter whether I call on Tuesday or Saturday, at noon or midnight. After this systematic series of experiments, Cerberus persists in having one more eye than I do, and I go gently. Ultimately, it's the dead connection I crave, Andy, not a living one. My cell phone has become like a Ouija board that promises the gateway into oblivion, manipulated into a sense of dialogue by nothing other than the nervous ticks of my fingers and the human impulse to control what cannot really be known. Death, in its insistence, is utterly respectable. The Deputy Sheriff is vulgar in his pulsing, responsive humanity, and I erase him.

Then the Decker Building, at 33 Union Square with you on the sixth floor and the Communist Party on the eighth. This is the spot where Valerie shot you. This is the elevator that saved Fred Hughes's life. Released on bail, she called to wish you a merry Christmas. She demanded a spot on Johnny Carson, publication of the *SCUM Manifesto*, and a bunch of cash. Do you wonder what possessed you to pick up the phone yourself, Andy?

All of this happened yesterday. It took less than an hour, and I have uncontrollably multiplied it in my mind so many times already. Is this how it was when you called Pat Hackett every morning? Dictating the diary entry for the previous day, keeping track of who you ran into and the cost of your cabs, such a thin line between an expense report and watching television with any given B over the telephone for hours at a time. Do you still call her up sometimes, just to screw with her? I think Ginsberg would.

There are other buildings. This is the number for Ginsberg. There is 860 Broadway, completely remodeled now, and 22 East 33rd Street, which no longer exists. This is the number for Errin. The shifting constellation of cellular mobility has not yet entirely supplanted the comforts of place. This is the number for Justin. There in the walls are phone jacks, tiny plastic tombstones marking the wires where your voice once ran. This is the number for you, Andy. You always said the telephone was your best friend.

Of Confessions During Blow Job

The weapon of choice for experimental filmmakers in 1963, a Bolex reel holds three minutes of sixteen-millimeter film. Nine reels at three minutes each is twenty-seven minutes of footage, divided by ten dollars a ticket, means I am paying about a buck a reel to sit here silently watching the black and white facial movements of a man on the receiving end of a blow job.

During the introduction to this little ditty of yours, Andy, the host says you have given us a great gift because when we give a blow job, we can't generally see what your camera is going to show us for the next half hour. The crowd laughs past the assumption that everyone in the crowd gives blow jobs. Real blow jobs, not metaphoric blow jobs. I look at my wife sitting next to me and think about her gold star.

Once while at a sex shop in Worcester looking for an appropriate souvenir, I found a copy of the classic *Debbie Does Dallas* on DVD. When I took it home, I discovered my wife had viewed only one other porno flick in her whole life. She'd never seen a money shot; bless her heart. When the team hits the showers and the jizz hits that cheerleader's eye, my wife flinched, shielding her eyes in a way that was funny but decidedly not in jest. So your movie is as close to the business end of a blow job as my wife will ever get, Andy.

The charge of obscenity has often been brought against you; this movie is not exceptional in that regard. Obscenity as a legal label has three components. First, the work must appeal to prurient interests, meaning: just how sexy is it? Second, the work must describe sexual conduct in an offensive way, meaning: just how common is a blow job? Third, the work must lack serious artistic merit, meaning: just how stupid are you, Andy? In short, the movie is clearly not obscene, but the label of obscenity is of course more loaded than any legal interpretation could suggest. You know it when you see it. You feel a secret. The compulsion to keep the secret a secret, not to let anybody come out with it. To keep it in the dark, a skeleton, a bone in the closet. Not to let it come, to keep a sin silent, to prevent it from being confessed.

Lights are at the top of the frame, heaven shining down on the head of this angel that we are expectantly searching for emotive clues. There is immediately nothing to see. The high lighting angle gives you the crown of his head and his nose, sometimes a bit of chin or wide cheekbone. His eyes are two giant black holes, his mouth a crooked strap of quietude. I think of a death mask and the specter of AIDS. What happened to this anonymous hustler when you were finished with him, Andy? How long did he live? The ghosts of ancient public service announcements are echoing and keening, straining against the dense fabric of silence in the theater. Did he dance himself out a window on speed? Did a john slash his throat and steal his wallet? Did he crash a car and bleed out on the road? Did he die of the mystery no doctor had yet named, poking at the lesions and wondering where he went wrong? My conviction that this young man is dead and that the death was unnatural, meaning: what is the relationship between your movie and this man's future?

It turns on you. Eventually, it turns you on. Everyone turns on, not for the reveal but for the conceal. Ultimately, and more intellectually, for the reveal of the conceal. The only person who has seen this entire movie, Andy, is you. When the screen whites out and we lose seven seconds while the new reel is being threaded, I think this must be where the action is. It happens eight times, always the head tilted back or the eyes rolling up or a new hint in the mouth, then the blindness. Seven seconds times eight reel changes is fifty-six seconds missing from this blow job, almost an entire minute where the subject knows quite well that you are not filming because you are replacing the reel. That amounts to four percent of the movie's total run time. I wonder if he waits to feel something genuinely personal until those three-minute marks. Would he do it out of self-consciousness or just to spite you? Did you ask the boys on their knees to halt a minute, or did you let them keep working him over?

How many boys were there? How often did they change places? Did you look only at the subject's face while filming, or did your eye inevitably wander lower? Andy, you are the only person who knows why the subject's face does what it does in this movie. You are the only person who has seen the blow job itself. Or are you? Were you even in the room, or did you just turn on the camera and walk out? Did you have an assistant there to change the reels for you? Did you excuse yourself, then return from the bathroom a few minutes later looking decidedly more relaxed? Everybody knows you like to watch, but how much of what exactly did you see?

The subject looks like a less chiseled version of James Dean. The hair just a little too tousled, the leather jacket with upturned collar, the Jim Stark broodingness of it all, the speedy living and the dead too soon. This movie promised us everything, Andy, but it's just a face. Pulled in off the street, he probably did it for ten bucks. In a parallel universe, this ten dollar bill is the same one I give to the geek behind the ticket counter to see your movie.

Really I thought the movie was quite sad, not in the particulars of the face, but in the sense that somewhere out there was this random young slice of anonymity mulling over the decision to participate, to say here is my painstaking effort to record a piece of the story of how I became so fucked up. I find the tricky thing is to be self-aware enough that you are letting the audience in on something important to you, but still keeping the audience out enough that you can satisfyingly and effectively use those very defenses of which you are making the audience aware. Sex sells, meaning: I am telling you that I know I use quickness of arched eyebrow and cruelty of curled lip as distancing tools, but I find this method preferable to XYZ other coping mechanisms and will continue to use it against you even though now you think you know me. You don't know me; you're turned on; I win; you've been hustled, turned. The best defense is a good offense.

So, you're stuck in a porno and can't get out of it. My favorite moment in this kind of confession is when one tries to preemptively deflect the I'm sorry that happened to you and corresponding here is the outpouring of what happened to me. After all, who among us has not been hustled? This is how hustlers are born. I do feel a kind of pity for this young man, and pity is worse than simple judging. And worse than pity sometimes is empathy. Don't think you know me because I have said this, and certainly don't think we are alike because you believe you have a story that resembles this one. But who has a story to tell like the subject of *Blow Job*? We sometimes fall into the trap of believing the grass is greener in another's psyche, but we are all still mowing the lawn with the same damn mower. We cope.

We take amphetamines drive real fast fuck for money get famous young witty die trying, and we lord it over each other because as long as I am telling you the dirtiest there is to know about me, you think you know me and you've got nothing on me. You are helpless in the grip of that universal question, meaning: what can I get for ten dollars? When in the Hotel Chelsea...

Either I am better than the man in the movie, or I am not better than the man in the movie. On one side of the coin, I am better or not better than the man. On the other side of the coin, nothingness, meaning: sometimes a blow job is just a blow job. Try not to think about it, right? We now refer to avant-garde filmmaking as independent, but it used to be called underground. Underground, meaning: buried, in general the opposite of fame. Then we have *Notes from Underground*, a confession of inactivity, of passively moving through life as one long blow job. The chronicle of a sex act that ultimately reveals to you your own boredom. There seems to be an awful lot riding on the achievement of this orgasm, Andy.

Dostoyevsky's novel had a hustler, too. The Underground Man gives and takes from Liza until she feels something less like tortured by and more like pity for this guy. He tries to give her a five ruble note, but she won't take it. He searches for her in the street and never finds her again. Nietzsche said it was one of his favorite books. How much of this matters if we can discern the identity of the subject in your movie, Andy? Was it DeVeren Bookwalter? There's this rumor going around that it was, and Willard Maas who got him off.

Among many greater accomplishments, Bookwalter also had a small role in the film *The Omega Man*, titled after that signature Nietzschean idea. Maas and his wife, filmmaker Marie Menken, were the inspiration for Edward Albee's horrifying play *Who's Afraid of Virginia Woolf?*, which premiered the year before *Blow Job*. Bookwalter died of stomach cancer at St. Vincent's in Manhattan in 1987. Maas died of a broken heart four days after his wife, who died of alcoholism in 1971. He was cremated; she was buried in the same cemetery as Gerard Malanga's dad. So the sordid tale is becoming clear, is coming out, is just coming. Now what, Andy? You win?

Ballad of the Maladies

Bioautography is the identification and comparison of any organic compound, separated by chromatography, through the study of its effect on living organisms. Some chemicals, vitamin B12 for example, have the ability to enhance growth in some organisms while retarding growth in others. I imagine lining up all your superstars' head shots across a sheet of cellulose paper. They are neat rows of tabs of acid, Andy, analytes bleeding out the sphinx of your influence across a chronogram.

Elisabeth Kübler-Ross once said that people are like stained glass windows. She is best known for introducing the five stages of grief in 1969. Do you know about this? The first stage is denial. I feel fine. This can't be happening. This can't be happening to me. Your father's death from liver disease in 1942. The jaundiced eyes and sallow skin, some said it was all his drinking and some said it was his gallbladder. The susceptibility of the gallbladder to disease is a hereditary trait. You are hiding under the bed. You are not going to the funeral. This is just Pittsburgh.

In twenty years, in New York now, this still can't be happening. In 1964, just before Halloween, Freddie Herko dances out an open window and splats onto Cornelia Street five stories below. He had been promising a suicide performance for weeks. Diane Di Prima says on the floor of his room, there is a book open to the page where a king leaps into the sea. We grasp for suicide notes. Freddie waits for the Sanctus in Mozart's *Coronation Mass*, playing on the hi-fi when they let him jump. There are two Saint Fredericks. One was stabbed to death and one was poisoned. In spring of 1966, Danny Williams' clothes are found in a pile next to his car, parked neatly by the coast of Cape Cod. The body is never found. Did he just walk into the sea, Andy? Daniel: Patron Saint of prisoners. You don't go to these funerals.

But on June 27, 1969, you are at 81st and Madison with twenty-two thousand other people filing past the coffin containing Judy Garland. Judy Garland: born Frances Ethel Gumm, age 47, accidental Seconal overdose. Frances: Patron Saint of motorists, orphans and immigrants. All your prints of Judy's head are the color of bruises. You are working, taping Ondine and Candy Darling as they wait to go past the casket. But Ondine is apparently taking sobriety seriously and not saying anything at all of interest. Candy is pulling more than her weight as only a drag queen can. In five years, her very own coffin will be here in this very same room, and you will not.

It begins like any other fever, progressing to delirium and abdominal pain, then diarrhea, intestinal hemorrhaging and even perforation of the ileum in the most dangerous stage. Typhoid is a bacteria transmitted by the ingestion of food or water contaminated by an infected person's shit. The most famous transmitter of this disease was Mary Mallon, a cook known to have infected at least 53 people, three of whom died from it. Typhoid Mary refused to stop working in kitchens, denying she had the disease right up until she died of pneumonia after twenty years under forcible quarantine. Mary was an asymptomatic carrier, meaning that she did not herself suffer what she inflicted on others. The autopsy revealed she still had live typhoid bacteria—want to guess where, Andy?—in her gallbladder. Mary: Mother of God, Blessed Virgin, Patron Saint of sailors and of cooks, against illness and against epidemics, and very many less ironic things.

The second stage is anger. Why do people keep dying around you? This is not fair. November 16, 1971: Edie Sedgwick, age 28, acute barbiturate intoxication. Both you and her fat cat family disowned her long before. You don't go to the funeral. Edith: Patron Saint of martyrs, and against the death of parents. August 8, 1972: Andrea Feldman, age 24, suicide by jumping out the 14th floor at 51 Fifth Avenue and 12th Street, holding a rosary in one hand and a Coca-Cola can in the other. Three weeks later, *Heat* came out and the significant role you gave her was positively reviewed. You don't go to the funeral. Andrea wasn't a saint at all.

Julia, on the other hand: Patron Saint against poverty and sickness. By your side and in your house each inch of the way until two years before she died, who you called every day of the nineteen months she was at Wightman Manor in Squirrel Hill, Julia Warhola, age 80. You don't go to your mother's funeral, Andy. And then March 21, 1974: Candy Darling, born James Lawrence Slattery, age 30, leukemia. Columbus Hospital is just a few blocks from your office and you never go to see her. *The New York Times* printed her obit on the front page. Candy was a darling, but not a saint. James the Lesser: Patron Saint of hat makers and wool cleaners. Everybody went to her funeral, except for you.

What do you say to get out of all these, Andy? Or have you done the dance for so long that you've been permanently excused? Not a joyful flowing, but an abnormal and involuntary movement disorder, a neurological complication occurring in twenty percent of children who catch rheumatic fever. Sydenham's Chorea, also known as Saint Vitus Dance, is primarily characterized by quick, uncoordinated jerking of the hands feet face. Vitus: Patron Saint of dance, of course. The most frequent psychiatric symptom is obsessive compulsive disorder. That's your number, surely. Julia kept you out of school because of cruel children, your body raging against itself, stuck in bed, fumbling with your scrapbook of autographed movie star head shots in neat little rows.

Motor coordination returning in due course, your neon skin retains the doodles of whatever dark frenzy your fingers briefly worked against their will in these deeply formative months. What could you give to get out of such a disease, Andy? This disease that watered and fed seedlings of nearly all the bedrock ideas you still cling to. The bones of one hand of Saint Vitus are in his cathedral in Prague, donated by the Duke of Bohemia. But there must be something to trade to want to pass right though adolescence in good health, to have a few more years as a regular kid. The third stage of grief is bargaining.

This is what you do on the floor of the office, Valerie Solanas getting into the elevator as you bleed out from the gaping hole in your chest. You were legally dead for six minutes. With whom did you make a deal, Andy? Eight vital organs, a corset forever, the tiny cups of pureed vegetables for lunch, more blood than shit. And if ever you should leave your house again without some pills of quietude, the vocabulary of sounds from a body quickly dying is horrifically vast. I know that ugly burble, have appraised that growl of bare life resonating unstoppably out from my own torn sack of meat. What price are you paying, Andy?

The fourth stage of grief is depression. Christmas Day, 1980: Gregory Battcock, age 43, stabbed 102 times. September 2, 1982: Tom Baker, age 42, accidental heroin overdose. October 2, 1982: Paul America, age 38, killed by car while walking home from the dentist. May 1983: Mickey Ruskin, age 50, heart attack complicated by cocaine addiction. August 1984: Truman Capote, age 59, liver disease complicated by multiple drug intoxication. 1985: Jackie Curtis, age 38, accidental heroin overdose. Ted Carey, age 53, illness complicated by AIDS. 1986: Tinkerbelle, age 40, suicide by jumping out a fifth floor window. Mario Amaya, age 52, illness complicated by AIDS. Jon Gould, age 33, illness complicated by AIDS. 1987: Ingrid Superstar, age unknown, went out for a pack of cigarettes and the body was never found.

A bonfire of your vanities, Andy, the Eighties were not easy on your kids. Raymond: Patron Saint of childbirth, and of the falsely accused. Typhoid Mary's ashes are buried in the Bronx at St. Raymond's. Acceptance is the final stage of grief. The hospital staff tried to resuscitate you for 45 minutes. You are dead at 6:31 on Sunday morning, February 22, 1987. A gallbladder you denied and deferred for decades, a Wednesday wake, a wrongful death suit settled for $3 million, an open casket of solid bronze with gold-plated rail and white upholstery, a Sotheby's estate auction grossing $20 million, a black cashmere suit and paisley tie, a Foundation for the Visual Arts, a platinum wig and sunglasses, a bottle of Estee Lauder's *Beautiful* perfume in your grave, a black prayer book and a single red rose in your hands.

Your public memorial mass is on April Fools Day. You don't go to it. Your body is decomposing in Pittsburgh, in the ground at St. John the Baptist: Patron Saint of lambs, of printers, of cutters. There are two meanings of cleave: to cut split sever separate sharply, or to attach agree associate adhere faithfully. Two thousand people are there. John Richardson says with bitterness that you are not meant to be your brother's keeper, then says with reverence that your special gift is detachment. You kind of hate Yoko, yet she is eulogizing you. Brigid Berlin reads the opening lines from The Book of Wisdom, Chapter 3, which begins, "but the souls of the just are in the hand of God, and no torment shall touch them."

Recurring Fear of Flat Champagne

The dream is silent, two fingers hovering across the mouth of justice. This is like Dustin Hoffman at the bottom of the swimming pool. Or it's my happening, and it's freaking me out. The central character lands full of purpose but completely empty of motivation in a town that looks like the set of *Lonesome Cowboys*. Short and shallow buildings are all some variation of sepia, hot soundless heat pressing out my footprints in dust.

I see myself, and therefore am not quite myself. The camera is here somewhere, a sturdy ladder and a bird's sharp eye patched with electrical tape. A direction to act natural is impossible to obey, everything having an out of control seemingness. Brightness falls as a pin in the corner of the scene held by my girl body covered in a lime and flamingo cheerleading uniform. Never in life have I worn such an outfit, evidence the central character is not the boss of the dream.

Cut to the doorway, to predestined destination that does not feel like what a goal feels like. Some kind of halfway house where a room waits for our girl, the door swings open as she raises a fist to knock. There stands the old woman. We have not been face to face in life, but it's only the familiarity that surprises. I know her features. She is blind. The useless brown eyes aim dumbly in my direction behind a pair of Ray-Bans, and her blotchy, diseased mouth contorts in one corner as though she is glad to smell me.

She is an ugly and devious blank on the outside. What's inside, Andy?

Cut to the woman hunched in an elevator, then down the short hallway, unlocking our girl's lodgings. We enter the room with no window, containing only a bed with classic threadbare quilt. The emptiness in the room seems unusual, but we don't worry because I have no baggage to unpack. Somehow time passes in the room with no window, and we are startled when I suddenly notice the woman in the doorway. How long she has been watching? What have I been doing while she is watching? Her presence indicates my soup is ready, though she gestures little and speaks not at all.

We retire for the evening. I sleep. Somehow time passes in the room with no window, and from where I lie in the bed we are startled when I notice the woman in the doorway. This image pops, tiny but clear, before darkness overtakes us again. I sleep.

In the morning I awaken with the sense that the image in the night was a dream. Only a dream, Andy, terrifying and harmless? Somehow the day passes. We have done work today but we don't know what kind or whether I have even left the halfway house. The woman in the doorway again. How long she has been watching? What have I been doing while she is watching? Soup. Somehow time passes. Sleep.

The pop is not the woman in the doorway this time. There is a pain in the bones of my left hand, moving its way to my wrist, a deep ache in the writing hand. It draws me out of sleep. I feel finally as if my hand is on fire. We are compelled to open our eyes and what is there at my hand is the woman.

A vague light from the crack in the door outlines the woman crouched by my bedside. Her mouth engulfs half my hand. I cannot move my fingers. I feel her yellow, uneven teeth grating against the palm of my writing hand. I can't move my legs, the thin quilt weighs down on me and I am paralyzed. We can see nothing clearly but her silver hair and her dead eyes in ecstasy and her mouth merged with the thin flesh of the backside of my hand. She catches the scent of our reaction and my sudden failed attempt at movement, and withdraws instantly. I am screaming as she does. There is no sound, but we are certain I am screaming. I cry silently and somehow time passes. Sleep.

In the morning I awaken with the sense this pop in the night was real. There is nothing wrong with my hand. Everything is as it was. We work again today and eat again today. Gradually this routine--we have no access to what it might be, but we feel it as a routine--calms us to the point where when the scene cuts quickly to my retiring again for the evening, we are authentically doe-eyed once more. Sleep.

There is a pain in the bones of my hand, moving its way to my wrist, drawing me out of sleep. We are compelled to open our eyes and what is there at my hand is the woman. A vague light from the crack in the door outlines the woman crouched by my bedside. Her mouth engulfs half my hand. I cannot move my fingers. I feel her yellow, uneven teeth grating against the palm of my writing hand. I can't move my legs, the thin quilt weighs down on me and I am paralyzed. We can see nothing clearly but her silver hair and her dead eyes in ecstasy and her mouth merged with the thin flesh of the backside of my hand. She catches the scent of our reaction and my sudden failed attempt at movement, and withdraws instantly. I am screaming as she does. There is no sound, but we are certain I am screaming. I cry silently and somehow time passes. Sleep.

In the morning we are certain this pop in the night is real. There is nothing wrong with my hand. We are surprised I have slept at all. The central character is increasingly distraught and cannot be calmed again. Inexplicably, work and soup occurs. Somehow time passes. We are shocked when the scene cuts immediately to me retiring for the evening. We desire to leave the halfway house but we cannot. Sleep.

The pain, it draws me out of sleep. We open our eyes to the woman. Her grating teeth, our paralysis. Pop. I cry silently and somehow time passes. Sleep. In the morning, we appeal to reality to please set in. We despair as the scene cuts immediately to my retiring for the evening. Sleep. The pain again. We are compelled to open our eyes though we are certain I slept with one eye open and what is there at my hand is you, Andy.

Your yellow, uneven teeth grate against the bones of my wrist as what is left of the nerves in my fingers touch the slick, spongy walls of your ghost throat. Your saliva burns my split knuckles and I am finally not paralyzed. As I withdraw my arm in panic from your ghost mouth my jagged fingernails get briefly caught. When both skins tear we feel it so deeply in our bones we think it may have made a noise. I kick you in your chest, scrambling out from under the quilt as your wig hits the floor. There is no sound, but we are certain I am screaming.

The camera goes down my ghost throat and when it pans backward out the shallow western town is gone, replaced by Manhattan. Cut to the top of the Union Square office in the night sky. We are moving quickly over the tops of tall buildings. The brightest thing in the universe--green and pink--we know what it is; I do not look down at it. The moon and stars light our way forward and sidewise. Do not look down. Do not look behind me. There is no sound, but we are certain you are there, Andy. You are chasing, your neon face hunting what parts of my writing hand may or may not be left. Why do I feel as if my arm is on fire? We jump from the top of one building to another. Max's Kansas City, Brownies. It seems like a cartoon. Or we are a video game. When my foot touches the roof I return immediately to the air.

You may be right behind us. You may already be long gone. I am moving quickly and do not look behind me. Time passes. Mary's, The Dom. Has the camera lost me? I no longer see myself jumping buildings. Time passes as the night sky becomes dawn. I am standing on top of St. Mark's Church and can hear the sound of the sun rising. Mark, who poured water that turned to wine, and into whose house a resurrected Christ came: Patron Saint of prisoners, a winged lion in the desert. If you disappear, Andy, how will you know?

me: What do you think about my book so far, Andy?

ghost: Oh, ah...it's great. It's really great.

me: Have you been reading it?

ghost: Not really. Uh, why? Have you been reading it?

me: I've been writing it.

ghost: Oh, great. Keep working, um...that's the best.

ABOUT THE AUTHOR

Megan Volpert is a poet and critic from Chicago who has settled in Atlanta with her wife, Mindy. Volpert holds an MFA in Creative Writing from Louisiana State University, and is a high school English teacher as well as a reviewer for Audible.

Sonics in Warholia is her fourth collection of poems. The other three are *The Desense of Nonfense* and *Face Blindness* (Buffalo: BlazeVOX Books, 2009 & 2007), and *Domestic Transmission* (San Antonio: MetroMania Press, 2007).

This self-proclaimed love child of Joan Jett and Roland Barthes has performed with a wide range of poets, from Christian Bök and Andrei Codrescu to Laura Mullen and Daphne Gottlieb. Volpert has been in competition at the National Poetry Slam, is a board member of Poetry Atlanta and is Co-Director of the Atlanta Queer Literary Festival with Collin Kelley.

Rooted in confessionalism and surrealism, her work has a strong interest in the performative and is also influenced by second-generation New York School poetry. Volpert is a theory junky and cannot resist rock and roll.

www.meganvolpert.com

ABOUT THE PUBLISHER

The mission of SIBLING RIVALRY PRESS is to develop, publish, and promote outlaw artistic talent - those projects which inspire people to read, challenge, and ponder the complexities of life in dark rooms, under blankets by cell-phone illumination, in the backseats of cars, and on spring-day park benches next to people studying Truman Capote and Andy Warhol. We welcome manuscripts which push boundaries, sing sweetly, or inspire us to perform karaoke in drag. Not much makes us flinch.

www.siblingrivalrypress.com

CPSIA information can be obtained at www.ICGtesting.com
Printed in the USA
LVOW101225240911

247697LV00001B/62/P